VALLEY OF
THE FAR SIDE

Other Books in The Far Side series

The Far Side
Beyond The Far Side
In Search of The Far Side
Bride of The Far Side
Hound of The Far Side
It Came from The Far Side
The Far Side Observer
Night of the Crash-Test Dummies
Wildlife Preserves
Wiener Dog Art
Unnatural Selections
Cows of Our Planet
The Chickens Are Restless
The Curse of Madame "C"

Anthologies

The Far Side Gallery
The Far Side Gallery 2
The Far Side Gallery 3
The Far Side Gallery 4
The Far Side Gallery 5

The PreHistory of The Far Side:
A 10th Anniversary Exhibit

VALLEY OF THE FAR SIDE

Gary Larson

WARNER BOOKS

A *Warner* Book

First published in Great Britain in 1987 by Futura Publications
Reprinted 1989, 1991
This edition published 1993 by Warner Books
Reprinted 1993, 1994, 1995

Copyright © 1980, 1981, 1982, 1983, 1984 by the Chronicle Publishing Company

The moral right of the author has been asserted

A CIP catalogue record of this book
is available from the British Library

ISBN 0 7515 0591 9

Printed and bound in Great Britain by
BPC Hazell Books Ltd
A member of
The British Printing Company Ltd

Warner Books
A Division of
Little, Brown and Company (UK)
Brettenham House
Lancaster Place
London WC2E 7EN

VALLEY OF THE FAR SIDE

Aerobics in hell

The Holsteins visit the Grand Canyon.

Unwittingly, Irwin has a brush with Death.

"Well, here's your problem, Mr. Schueler."

6

"I'm leaving you, Frank, because you're a shiftless, low-down, good-for-nothing imbecile . . . and, might I finally add, you have the head of a chicken."

"Well, we might as well put it on board—although I'm not sure what use we'll have for a box of rusty nails, broken glass, and throwing darts."

"Take this handkerchief back to the lab, Stevens. I want some answers on which monster did this—Godzilla? Gargantua? Who?"

Animal nerds

8

"OK, listen up! The cops are closing in on this place, so here's our new hideout: 455 Elm Street.... Let's all say it together about a hundred times so there'll be no screw-ups."

"OK, one more time and it's off to bed for the both of you.... 'Hey, Bob. Think there are any bears in this old cave?' ... 'I dunno, Jim. Let's take a look.'"

"Watch ... Thag says he make gravel angel."

10

"Oh! Wait! Wait! My mistake! . . . That's him down there!"

One remark led to another, and the bar suddenly polarized into two angry, confrontational factions: those espousing the virtues of the double-humped camel on the one side, single-humpers on the other.

"Well, Mr. Cody, according to our questionnaire, you would probably excel in sales, advertising, slaughtering a few thousand buffalo, or market research."

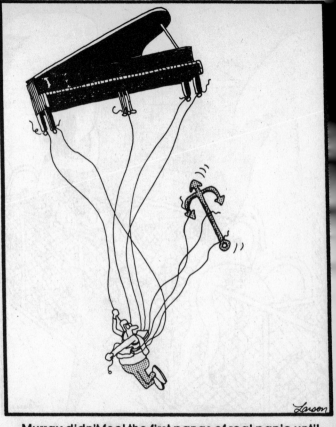

Murray didn't feel the first pangs of real panic until he pulled the emergency cord.

12

"Harold! The dog's trying to blow up the house again!
Catch him in the act or he'll never learn."

"It's OK! It's OK! The tunnel was closing in on me there
for a while, but I'm all right now."

"Thag, take napkin. Got some mammoth on face."

Mrs. Flemming's GORILLA FINISHING SCHOOL

"The boss wants his money, see? Or next time it won't be just your living room we rearrange."

"Bear! Bear!"

"Ha! Ain't a rattler, Jake. You got one of them maraca players down your bag—and he's probably more scared than you."

"Bob! Wake up! Bob! A ship! I think I see a ship! . . . Where are your glasses?"

16

"Oh, I see! You return covered with blond feathers, and I'm supposed to believe you crossed the road *just* to get to the other side?"

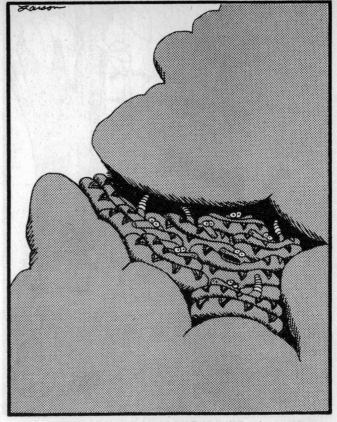

"Hey, I feel someone moving! Dang, this place gives me the willies."

How birds see the world

"Hey! I'm gonna roll now! You guys gonna watch or what?"

"Oh, Laaaaaarrrrrry ... I think you should look up niiiiiice and eaaaaasy and see what's right ... over ... your ... head."

The restless life of the nomad

"Sorry about this, buddy, but the limit on those things is half a dozen—looks like you're one over."

The young dog's nightmare: premature mange

Fly heaven

Suddenly, Bobby felt very alone in the world.

"I don't seeeeee . . . Wait! There it is! Oo! I hate those little slivers that stand straight up and down."

"Well, we've tried every device and you still won't talk—every device, that is, except this little baby we simply call 'Mr. Thingy.'"

The anthropologist's dream: A beautiful woman in one hand, the fossilized skull of a *Homo habilus* in the other

Ginger decides to take out Mrs. Talbot's flower bed once and for all.

"Gee . . . look at all the little black dots."

"And here he is—but when I started, I bet he was at least this tall."

When animal mimicry breaks down

26

"Dang! Get my shotgun, Mama! The aliens are after the chickens again."

"Well this shouldn't last too long."

27

"Excuse me, but I'm trying to sleep next door and all I hear is scratching, clawing, and 'eek, eek, eek.'"

Vending machines of the Serengeti

"Now remember—roar just as you leap.... These things have some of the greatest expressions."

Hour after hour, cup after cup, the two men matched their caffeine limits in a traditional contest of the Old West.

"Well, heaven knows what it is or where it came from—just get rid of it. But save that cheese first."

"Come and get it! Cooooome and get it! . . . It's not going to get any more raw, y'know."

The third most common cause of forest fires

"My next guest, on the monitor behind me, is an organized crime informant. To protect his identity, we've placed him in a darkened studio—so let's go to him now."

"Hey . . . Be cool, man, be cool."

32

"Remember me, Mr. Schneider? Kenya. 1947. If you're going to shoot at an elephant, Mr. Schneider, you better be prepared to finish the job."

"Hey, thank you! Thank you! That was 'Tie a Yellow Ribbon.' . . . Now, what say we all *really* get down?"

"Ha ha ha, Biff. Guess what? After we go to the drugstore and the post office, *I'm* going to the vet's to get tutored."

"Shh. Listen! There's more: 'I've named the male with the big ears Bozo, and he is surely the nerd of the social group—a primate bimbo, if you will.'"

"Well, shucks! I've lost again. Talk about your alien luck!"

"Let's see here. . . . Oh! Close, but no cigar. You want the place up the road—same as I told those other fellahs."

The origin of "dessert"

**"Now just hold your horses, everyone.... Let's let it run
for a minute or so and see if it gets any colder."**

Okay, mom, I see you, I see you...

"Bedtime, Leroy. Here comes your animal blanket."

"It's the mailman, doc. He scares me."

"You gotta check this out, Stuart. Vinnie's over on the couch putting the moves on Zelda Schwartz—but he's talkin' to the wrong end."

"Hold on there! I think you misunderstood—I'm Al Tilley . . . the bum."

"Uh-oh, I've got a feeling I shouldn't have been munching on these things for the last mile."

Suddenly the burglars found themselves looking
down the barrel of Andy's Doble-o-matic.

40

"Well, it just sort of wriggled its way up the beach, grabbed Jonathan, and dragged him back again. I mean, the poor thing must have been half-starved."

Circa 1500 A.D.: Horses are introduced to America.

41

"Just stay in the cab, Vern . . . maybe that bear's hurt, and maybe he ain't."

"Dang it, Monica! I can't live this charade any longer! I'm not a telephone repairman who stumbled into your life—I'm a Komodo dragon, largest member of the lizard family and a filthy liar."

43

Fire is invented.

The Vikings, of course, knew the importance of
stretching before an attack.

barn
door

farmer
bob

"So when Farmer Bob comes through the door, three
of us circle around and ... Muriel! ... Are you
chewing your cud while I'm talking?"

"Oh, is that so? Well, you might be a kangaroo, but I know a few things about marsupials *myself*!"

"OK, he's asleep. Pull the wagon, Buck, and I'll start barkin' my head off. . . . God, I love this."

"Oh, quit worrying about it, Andrew. They're just love handles."

Unfortunately, Larry had always approached from the side that wasn't posted, and a natural phenomenon was destroyed before anyone could react.

Cheetah wheelies

"One more thing, young man. You get my daughter home before sunrise—I don't want you coming back here with a pile of dried bones."

French mammoth

"Well, somehow they knew we were—whoa! Our dorsal fins are sticking out! I wonder how many times *that's* screwed things up?"

Einstein discovers that time is actually money.

49

How nature says, "Do not touch."

"There it is—the old Muffy place. They say on some nights, when the moon is full, you can still hear him dragging his chain to the old oak and back."

As Thak worked frantically to start a fire, a
Cro-Magnon man, walking erect, approached the
table and simply gave Theena a light.

"Yes! That's right! The answer *is* 'Wisconsin!' Another 50 points for God, and ... uh-oh, looks like Norman, our current champion, hasn't even scored yet."

"Well, that cat's doing it again. Keeping that poor thing alive just to play with it awhile."

"Oh, wow! How could you even *think* that, Wendy? Of *course* it's your mind I'm attracted to!"

Although an unexplained phenomenon, there is a place on the outskirts of Mayfield, Nebraska, where the sun does not shine.

The perils of improper circling

"Wait just a gol dang minute here! He's been dealin' from the bottom of the deck, Jake! My pappy always said, 'Never trust a grizzly.'"

"Well, I suppose you're all wondering why I've asked you here today. . . . Ha! I've always wanted to say that."

"Boy, I'm sooooo full, and this is the laaaaast slice of beef . . . guess I'll finish it off, though."

"Well, I laid four Wednesday, three yesterday, and two more today ... of course, George keeps saying we shouldn't count them until they hatch."

How entomologists pass away

"Whoa, back off, Bobby Joe. That's just your reflection."

"Whoa, back off, bobby. You, that's just your reflection!"

"OK, Baxter, if that's your game, I'll just reach over and push a few of *your* buttons."

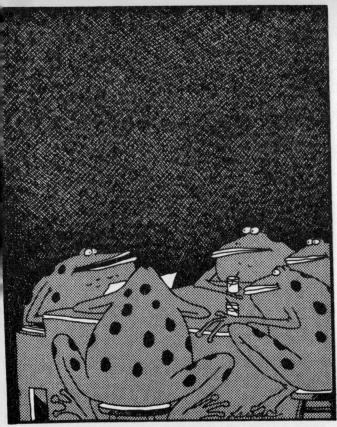

"OK. Here's another little ditty we can all sing.... Of course, as always, the only words are 'ribbit, ribbit.'"

At the Dog Comedy Film Festival

59

When snakes trip

"Well, so that's it.... I thought he was coming up awfully easy."

"Well, Vern, looks like that buffalo paper you set out this morning is doing the trick."

"Hey, Sid! Remember that time last summer we were all gathered around the kill like this, someone told a leopard joke, and you laughed so hard an antler came out your nose?"

Birds of prey know they're cool.

"Aw, c'mon, you guys—the cat's away and everyone's so dead serious."

"Well, the Parkers are dead. . . . You had to encourage them to take thirds, didn't you?"

"Well, I've got your final grades ready, although I'm afraid not everyone here will be moving up."

"Hey! I think you've hit on something there! Sheep's clothing! Sheep's clothing! . . . Let's get out of these gorilla suits!"

"Look at this mob. We'll be lucky if there's a seat cushion left."

"Well, I don't think so, but I'll ask. Hey, Arlene! Anyone turn in a human brain left here yesterday? . . . He says it was medium-sized, sort of pinkish."

Toe, heel, toe, heel, toe, toe... No. Wait... Toe, heel, heel... Dang! I think I just wasted fifty bucks.

JUMBO TAP SHOES

"You idiot! I said get the room freshener! That's the insecticide!"

As the smallest member of the gang, Wendall was used as an attention-getter while cruising for girls.

"Well, I guess that ain't a bad story—but let me tell you about the time I lost *this*!"

"Cummings! Schneider! You've got plenty of research to work on ... and for the last time stop playing with those plastic models!"

"Oh, this should be interesting.... Looks as if your father has forgotten about the front window again."

How vampires have accidents

Neanderthal creativity

"I beg your pardon, but you're not planning just to throw that fly away, are you?"

"Gad, it gives me the creeps when he does that. I swear that goldfish is possessed or something."

"Well, we must face a new reality. No more carefree days of chasing squirrels, running through the park, or howling at the moon. On the other hand, no more 'Fetch the stick, boy, fetch the stick.'"

"What is this? . . . Some kind of cruel hoax?"

"Hold on there, Dale. It says we should sand between coats."

The modern lion

Deep inside, Brian wondered if the other guys really listened to his ideas or regarded him only as comic relief.

Roger screws up.

"The fuel light's on, Frank! We're all going to die!...
We're all going to die!... Wait, wait.... Oh, my
mistake—that's the intercom light."

"See how the vegetation has been trampled flat
here, Jimmy? That tells me where a deer bedded
down for the night. After a while, you'll develop an
eye for these things yourself."

74

Ed and Barbara are visited by the insects of the
Amazon Basin.

"Now you listen to me, Miss Billings! You have not seen a thing here—do you understand? I'm not kidding about this, Miss Billings."

Creationism explained

The termite queen in her egg chamber

Disaster befalls Professor Schnabel's cleaning lady when she mistakes his time machine for a new dryer.

77

"Get, you rascal! Get! ... Heaven knows how he keeps getting in here, Betty, but you better count 'em."

How locusts are incited to swarm

"As if we all knew where we're going."

"Shoot! You not only got the wrong planet, you got the wrong *solar* system... I mean, a wrong planet I can understand—but a whole solar system?"

"It's the Websters. They say there's some pitiful thing dying of thirst out their way, and would we like to come over?"

"No way. I'll put *my* magazine down when you put yours down."

"Doreen! There's a spider on you! One of those big, hairy, brown ones with the long legs that can move like the wind itself!"

"Details are still sketchy, but we think the name of the bird sucked into the jet's engines was Harold Meeker."

"Watch out for that tree, you idiot! . . . And *now* you're on the wrong side of the road. Criminy! You're driving like you've been pithed or something."

"You know, I have a confession to make, Bernie. Win or lose, I love doing this."

"Great . . . Just great, you imbecile! I've been floating here for hours like a harmless log and *you* come up and start talking to me!"

"Listen! The authorities are helpless! If the city's to be saved, I'm afraid it's up to us! *This is our hour!*"

"Criminy! Kevin's oozing his way up onto the table....
Some slugs have a few drinks and just go nuts!"

Toby vs. Godzilla

Danny shows off his sheep's brain.

"Hey, Barry—in the back row—new kid."

"*Now* that desk looks better. Everything's squared away, yessir, squaaaaaared away."

"Well, here comes Roy again. He sure does think he's Hell on Wheels."

How snakes say goodbye

"Aaaaaa! Here they come again, Edgar! . . . Crazy carnivores!"

"Bob! You fool.... Don't plug that thing in!"

"Look, just relax, son... relaaaaaaaax... I'm gonna come over there now and you can just hand me your gun.... Everything's gonna be reeeal cool, son."

"Now, in this slide we can see how the cornered cat has seemed to suddenly grow bigger.... Trickery! Trickery! Trickery!"

"... four ... five ... six ... Oh, what the hell—just turn and shoot."

When cliff divers belly flop

"No doubt about it, Ellington—we've mathematically
expressed the purpose of the universe. Gad, how I
love the thrill of scientific discovery!"

"Just back off, buddy . . . unless you want a fat lip."

"Hank! You're reflecting!"

"Hey, hey, hey! Are you folks nuts? I'm telling you, *this* is the car for you."

"All right! All right! If you want the truth, off and on I've been seeing *all* the vowels—a, e, i, o, u.... Oh, yes! And *sometimes* y!"

"*There's* one of 'em! ... And I think there are at least three or four more runnin' around in here!"

"For crying out loud, gentlemen! That's us! Someone's installed the one-way mirror in backward!"

"Dad! Find out if they have cable!"

"Civilization-slickers."

"You're on. Ten to one if I start howling I'll have everyone here howling inside five minutes."

"That's right, the forty-ninth floor.... And you better hurry—she's hanging by a thread."

Just look at all those stars, Becky... There must be hundreds of 'em!

Carl Sagan as a kid

"And I suppose *you* think this is a dream come true."

"Well, every dog has his day."

"Oh yeah? More like the three wise guys, I'd say."

"Here, Fifi! C'mon! . . . Faster, Fifi!"

Ship of Fools

Car of Idiots

Early experiments in transportation

"Bob, do you think I'm sinking? Be honest."

"Foster! You better get over here if you want to see Johnson's hangnail magnified 500 times."

"Wendell . . . I'm not content."

103

"And as the net slooooooowly lifted him from the
water, the voice kept whispering, 'I want your legs....
I want your legs.'"

Other titles by Gary Larson.
To order these or other Warner titles, please see the following page

All Gary Larson's titles published by Warner Books can be ordered from the following address:

Little, Brown and Company (UK),
P.O. Box 11,
Falmouth,
Cornwall TR10 9EN.

Alternatively you may fax your order to the above address.
Fax No. 01326 317444

Payments can be made as follows: cheque, postal order (payable to Little, Brown and Company) or by credit cards, Visa/Access. Do not send cash or currency. UK customers and B.F.P.O. please allow £1.00 for postage and packing for the first book, plus 50p for the second book, plus 30p for each additional book up to a maximum charge of £3.00 (7 books plus).

Overseas customers including Ireland, please allow £2.00 for the first book, plus £1.00 for the second book, plus 50p for each additional book.

NAME (Block Letter) ....

ADDRESS ....

....

☐ I enclose my remittance for _____

☐ I wish to pay by Access/Visa Card

Number | | | | | | | | | | | | | | | |

Card Expiry Date | | | | |